Who Is Chloe Kim?

by Stefanie Loh

illustrated by Manuel Gutierrez

Penguin Workshop

To my wife, Lauren, and my family—
you all make me feel like I can do anything—SL

To Deborah & Lisa—MG

PENGUIN WORKSHOP
An imprint of Penguin Random House LLC, New York

First published in the United States of America by Penguin Workshop,
an imprint of Penguin Random House LLC, New York, 2022

Visit us online at penguinrandomhouse.com.

Library of Congress Cataloging-in-Publication Data is available.

Printed in the United States of America

ISBN 9780593519691 (paperback)   10 9 8 7 6 5 4 3 2 1 WOR
ISBN 9780593519707 (library binding)   10 9 8 7 6 5 4 3 2 1 WOR

Contents

Who Is Chloe Kim?

On February 13, 2018, seventeen-year-old Chloe Kim skidded to a halt at the bottom of the half-pipe course at the PyeongChang (say: pee-YONG-chang) Winter Olympics and, in disbelief, grabbed her helmet with both hands, a giant grin on her face. She *knew* she'd stomped that run! It was the third and final attempt in her quest for her first Olympic medal while in South Korea. Someone handed the Korean American snowboarding sensation a US flag, and she spread it out behind her like a cape, staring hopefully at the scoreboard and waiting for the result of her final run to come in.

It finally flashed onto the big screen: 98.25! Chloe pumped her fists triumphantly, still holding the corners of the flag as she hopped up and down in excitement! She'd done it! The gold medal was hers.

One of Chloe's Team USA teammates ran up to give her a big hug. The moment that Chloe had spent years training for was here, and pride filled the teenager as she thought about what she'd accomplished. In the country her parents were from, in front of many Korean family members, Chloe had delivered. Chloe Kim had lived up to all the expectations placed upon her since she'd announced herself to the snowboarding world at age thirteen. Now she had become the youngest American woman to ever medal in snowboarding at the Olympics—and she'd done it in style, pulling off a trick that had never been done by a woman before at the Olympic Games.

"When you work for something for so long and you go home with the best possible outcome, it's amazing," Chloe said later, at her victory press conference. "Today, I really did it for my family," she said as her parents watched proudly from the back of the room.

In some ways, Chloe's electrifying performance at the PyeongChang Winter Olympics in 2018 was the storybook ending to the unlikely tale of how a Korean American girl, who grew up in a Korean immigrant family of nonathletes, became a gold-medal-winning Winter Olympian and a role model for many in the Asian American community. But in other ways, it merely served as an introduction. Because as a seventeen-year-old at her first Winter Olympics, Chloe's Olympic snowboarding career was really just beginning.

CHAPTER 1
From Korea to America

Chloe Kim was born in Torrance, California, on Easter Sunday, April 23, 2000. She is a first-generation Korean American, which means that her father, Jong Jin Kim, and her mother, Boran Yun Kim, were both born outside the United States but moved to America before they had Chloe. Jong Jin moved from South Korea to the United States in 1982, carrying a Korean-English dictionary and $800 in cash. He picked Los Angeles as his destination because that was the only direct flight he could afford. He thought of America as his dream country and a land of opportunity.

With his $800, Jong Jin bought an inexpensive car and paid $150 for a weeklong stay at a motel.

Then he found work as a dishwasher at a burger restaurant and also as a cashier at a store. He practiced English with his customers at work as he saved up money so he could go to college. Soon, Jong Jin was studying engineering at El Camino College by day while working at night as a machinery operator, to put himself through school. He worked as an engineer after college and met his first wife. They had two daughters together—Tracy and Erica—but the marriage did not last. After they divorced, Jong Jin moved to Switzerland, where his older sister lived. That's where he met Chloe's mom, Boran, when she was in town on a business trip. They fell in love, got married in 1998, and moved to California, where they had Chloe.

When Chloe was only four years old, Jong Jin took her snowboarding for the first time. They drove to Mountain High, a small ski resort in the San Gabriel Mountains, about two hours from their house. Father and daughter learned to snowboard together, but Chloe showed more natural talent than her dad. By the time she was five, Chloe was hitting small jumps and rails on a board that Jong Jin had bought online for twenty-five dollars. The little girl in the pink jacket and purple snowboarding pants rode fearlessly, always bouncing up eagerly to try again after every spill.

Even though he didn't know very much about snowboarding in the beginning, Jong Jin encouraged Chloe's love for her new hobby and tried to come up with new ways to help her improve. Chloe's dad was her first coach. "I think his engineering background helped a lot," Chloe has said. "Thinking about what you need to do to spin and all that stuff." When she first started, Chloe rode most naturally with her right foot forward on her snowboard. But whenever possible, Jong Jin encouraged his daughter to ride "switch," which meant leading with her left leg forward.

It felt strange at first, and it wasn't easy, but Jong Jin persisted, believing that it would help Chloe develop both sides of her body and make it easier for her to do difficult tricks. Today, after years of practice, Chloe is one of the best switch riders in the snowboarding world.

To keep Chloe safe and make falling on snow hurt less, Jong Jin cut up his wife's old yoga mats and stuffed them into his daughter's snowboarding pants as cushioning. When Jong Jin heard that waxed snowboards would go faster, he melted candles onto the bottom of Chloe's snowboard, hoping that would give her a little boost. (As it turns out, candle wax and snowboard wax aren't quite the same thing—the board cracked after Chloe's first run!)

When Chloe was six years old, she joined the Mountain High snowboarding team, mostly because it made snowboarding lessons a little cheaper. By the end of her first season, she was invited to compete at the United States of America Snowboard and Freeski Association (USASA) nationals in Lake Tahoe, on the border of California and Nevada.

Making nationals was a big deal! Jong Jin and Chloe drove eight hours to Lake Tahoe only to find that every hotel room in the area was already booked. They ended up sleeping in their car. But that didn't stop Chloe from getting her first taste of snowboarding success at the national level— she won three bronze medals in her age group. A year later, she competed at nationals again and won her first junior national championship.

CHAPTER 2
Nugget of an Olympic Dream

Chloe was eight when her parents sent her to live with her aunt in Geneva, Switzerland, for two years. The move was Jong Jin's idea because, in addition to the English that Chloe

learned at school in America and the Korean her parents taught her at home, he wanted Chloe to learn to speak French. "People think Chloe moved to Switzerland for snowboarding, but we are not athletes," Jong Jin later said. "Her education was important. Sometimes I hear people say education is the backup plan. They have it backwards. Education is the life plan."

Chloe started third grade in Switzerland and realized she was the only Asian girl at her school. At first, she felt out of place. Some of the other kids bullied her, making mean comments about her almond-shaped eyes. "Where are you from? And what are you?" her classmates would ask. These questions made Chloe start thinking about her identity as a girl of Korean ethnicity who was born in America to parents who had emigrated from Korea. She answered her Swiss classmates by saying, "I'm a California girl. I'm from Los Angeles." To her Swiss classmates, Los Angeles was where celebrities and movie stars lived, and they decided that this made Chloe cool. As she learned to speak French and could communicate better with the other kids, things improved for Chloe.

Chloe continued her snowboarding training while in Switzerland. She joined the Swiss snowboarding team in third grade and learned how to do complicated twists off the half-pipe. A half-pipe is the U-shaped tube covered in smooth snow that freestyle snowboarders compete on, using the walls to launch different tricks. At age nine, Chloe had already learned how to do McTwists—a trick that involves flipping forward off the lip of the half-pipe and performing one and a half rotations.

During Chloe's two years in Switzerland, her parents took turns coming to visit. When Jong Jin visited Chloe, they often went snowboarding. One summer, he took her to Snowpark Zermatt, where many professional snowboarders train. While watching Chloe among the other snowboarders there, Jong Jin noticed one woman landing challenging tricks. He started talking to her coach and was surprised when he learned that the woman had finished tenth in the 2006 Winter Olympics in Turin, Italy. When he watched his daughter and the Olympian practice together on their snowboards, Jong Jin realized that Chloe could be at that level in two years.

When Jong Jin returned to California after his visit to Switzerland, he told his wife, "I can bring Chloe to the Olympics." Boran believed him. Jong Jin decided to quit his job as an engineer to support Chloe in her emerging snowboarding career. But it wasn't just Jong Jin who was excited about Chloe's snowboarding skills. By the time Chloe was about ten years old, she had fallen in love with snowboarding and decided that it was something she wanted to do for the rest of her life.

Chloe moved back to the United States in 2010 and started training with the Mammoth Mountain snowboarding team. This was a big commitment because Mammoth Mountain, in central California, was a five-and-a-half-hour drive from the Kims' Southern California home. But it had a better snowboarding team than the one Chloe used to compete for at Mountain High.

The long drive to and from Mammoth became a regular part of the Kims' lives. Boran would stay up late at night cooking and packing meals for her husband and daughter to take on their journey. Then, on Fridays, Jong Jin would wake up at 2:00 a.m., carry Chloe from her bed to the back seat of the car, and drive them all the way to Mammoth for Chloe to train with her new team.

CHAPTER 3
The Future of Snowboarding

Olympic gold medalist Kelly Clark was standing in line to get on the ski lift at Mammoth Mountain one day in 2009 when she felt a tug on the sleeve of her snowboarding jacket. Kelly looked down to see a little girl in a blue helmet and pink face mask standing behind her. It was eight-year-old Chloe. "Are you Kelly Clark?" she asked shyly, awed to be in the presence of a snowboarding legend. "She . . . asked to go up the lift with me. It was pretty cute," said Kelly, who was about twenty-six at the time. Over the next few years, Kelly became a mentor to Chloe and tried to help the younger girl wherever she could. She was perhaps one of the first people to really see Chloe as the future of snowboarding.

By the time she was in eighth grade in 2013, Chloe's snowboarding career was taking off. She had decided to go professional at age thirteen, had made the US Snowboarding team, and was now a teammate of Kelly's.

Even as Kelly and Chloe competed at international-level snowboarding events, they stayed friends and pushed each other.

In December 2013, at the Dew Tour iON Mountain Championships in Breckenridge, Colorado, Chloe finished third in women's superpipe—just one point behind Kelly, who came in second. Australia's Torah Bright, another idol of Chloe's, won the gold medal. Chloe was ecstatic to stand on the winner's podium next to her childhood snowboarding heroes, Kelly and Torah. But the thing that left the snowboarding community buzzing that day was how Chloe's third place finish at the Dew Tour—an Olympic team selection event— meant that her score would have qualified her for the 2014 Winter Olympics in Sochi, Russia! Unfortunately, Chloe wasn't eligible to participate. To compete in snowboarding at the Olympic Games, athletes have to be fifteen years old at the start of the competition. When the 2014 Winter Olympics began on February 7 in Sochi, Chloe was still a couple of months shy of her fourteenth birthday.

In the end, that wouldn't matter—2014 was the year that Chloe announced herself to the snowboarding world. In January, at her first X Games in Aspen, Colorado, Chloe became the youngest person to ever win an X Games medal when she finished second in the women's superpipe.

The following year, Chloe made history again when she became the youngest person to ever win an X Games gold medal. Her win over Kelly and Torah was a big deal because the two older women had medaled at the 2014 Winter Olympics—Torah took the silver medal home to Australia, while Kelly clinched bronze for Team USA. It made everyone wonder if Chloe might have won a medal if she'd been old

enough to compete in the Olympics the year before.

With a second-straight gold medal at the 2016 X Games, Chloe became the first athlete in X Games history to win back-to-back gold medals and three total medals before the age of sixteen. But she was just getting started.

On February 6, 2016, in Park City, Utah, for the US Snowboarding Grand Prix, Chloe landed the trick that would become her signature move and make her a snowboarding legend. She had already sewed up the gold medal that day, thanks to a 96.5 score on her first of three runs. Then, on her final run, she dropped into the half-pipe and glided down the wall, cruising up and out onto the opposite lip till she was airborne, high above the snow. She dropped back down onto the pipe, gaining speed as she steered her board back up the front wall. Airborne again, Chloe executed three tight twists, wowing the crowd as she stuck the landing and rode her board effortlessly toward the opposite wall.

"There's a 1080 right there," the excited television announcers exclaimed. That in itself was big. A 1080 is an advanced trick in which the snowboarder has to launch into the air and complete three full-body rotations before landing. It had taken years before women snowboarders had managed to pull it off. (Kelly had performed the first 1080 in competition at the 2011 X Games.)

But fresh off that impressive 1080 launched off the front wall of the half-pipe, Chloe sped up the back wall and powered herself through the air. She grabbed the end of her board and spun. Once. Twice. Three times. "OHHHHHHHHHHHHH," the TV announcers exclaimed as Chloe landed safely on the pipe. "Ladies and gentlemen, you have just witnessed history!" the excited announcers

declared as Chloe slid to the finish and was met by a grinning Kelly, who gave Chloe a big congratulatory hug. Chloe had just become the only woman to *ever* land back-to-back 1080s in a snowboarding competition. Her reward? A perfect score of one hundred from the judges!

A week after she landed her history-making trick, Chloe waved the US flag proudly as she led Team USA during the opening ceremony at the 2016 Winter Youth Olympic Games in Lillehammer, Norway. Chloe went on to win gold medals in the half-pipe and slopestyle snowboarding events. (In slopestyle snowboarding, athletes ride a course that consists of rails, jumps, and other obstacles. They're scored on the difficultly of their tricks, how high in the air they get on the obstacles, and how well they perform tricks.)

Chloe's Youth Olympics success completed

her arrival in the world of international snowboarding. This girl, everyone agreed, would be the one to watch at the 2018 Winter Olympics in PyeongChang, South Korea.

CHAPTER 4
2018 Winter Olympics

Chloe locked up her spot in the 2018 Winter Olympics in December 2017 when she won the Dew Tour, an Olympic-qualification event in Breckenridge, Colorado. But it wasn't until after the competition that Chloe's accomplishment really hit her: "I'm going to the Olympics!" Chloe said excitedly in interviews with journalists afterward. "It seems like a dream almost, and I'm just trying to wake up."

That her first Olympics would take place in her parents' home country of South Korea wasn't lost on Chloe. The location of the 2018 Winter Olympics was originally announced in 2011, and even then, it had cemented Jong Jin's belief in his daughter's destiny. Everything in her life had lined up to deliver her here, he thought.

Chloe was born in 2000, which, in the Chinese zodiac, is the year of the dragon. But according to Korean myth, a dragon is not born a dragon. It starts life as a big snake, then waits a thousand years, and on a stormy day, it goes up into the sky and becomes a full dragon. *Imugi* is the Korean word for baby dragon. Jong Jin called Chloe *ipugi*—a made-up Korean word meaning "baby girl dragon." Instead of waiting a thousand years to blossom into a dragon, Chloe had to wait four. Could Chloe's return to the land of her ancestors to compete in the PyeongChang Winter Olympics be the moment she fulfilled her destiny and rose to the skies to become a real dragon?

Folklore of the dragon aside, the PyeongChang Winter Olympics were special for Chloe because she would get to represent both the Korean and American sides of her identity. A full year

before the Olympics, Chloe flew to Seoul in February 2017 on behalf of the US State Department to speak at news conferences full of Korean media. Her father had arranged some of these events to introduce Chloe to a country where she was still largely unknown.

On that trip, Chloe spoke to Korean journalists in fluent Korean, telling them that her Korean name was Kim Sun, naming some of her favorite Korean music artists (K-pop star CL) and her favorite Korean foods (tteokbokki—spicy rice cakes). She met with Korean Olympians, taught Korean kids to snowboard, and spent time with her extended family. The Koreans fell in love with the snowboarding star who competed for the United States but looked like them.

Chloe thought a lot about her identity as a Korean American athlete in the lead-up to the 2018 Olympics. As a child, she had often felt like she never really fit in. People would ask her questions like "Why is your English so good?" and she was not quite sure what to say. She even went through a period as a young teenager when she stopped speaking Korean to her parents in public because the racism she had experienced from being in the spotlight made her secretly feel ashamed to be Asian. Yet at the same time, she felt guilty about having those feelings.

But as she answered more questions about what it was like to be a Korean American snowboarder competing for Team USA in her parents' home country, Chloe embraced both sides of her heritage with pride. "I have this different opportunity because I'm Korean American but I'm riding for the States," she has said. "At first I was confused on how that would be accepted. But now I'm starting to understand that I can represent both countries. I have a Korean face. But I was born and raised in the States."

On February 13, 2018, the morning of the women's half-pipe final at the PyeongChang Olympics, Jong Jin texted his daughter: "Hey Ipugi, today is your day to become a dragon." He was right. At Phoenix Snow Park, Jong Jin, Boran, and Chloe's two sisters all gathered at the bottom of the hill that the half-pipe was built into to cheer on Chloe. Chloe's aunt had flown in from Switzerland for the big moment. Five South Korean relatives, including Chloe's seventy-five-year-old grandma who had never seen her compete live, had all come to watch. They held signs that read "Go, Chloe Kim!" in Korean and English.

Chloe crushed the competition on her first run, scoring a 93.75 that included the always challenging 1080 and put her in first place. On her second run, Chloe went bigger. She tried to land back-to-back 1080s—which no one had ever done before at the women's half-pipe in the

Olympics—but couldn't quite nail the landing on the second one. Still, her first run had been good enough that going into her final attempt, Chloe was already a lock for the gold medal. This was really a victory lap. But that's not how Chloe saw it. "I knew if I went home with a gold medal knowing I could do better, I wouldn't be very satisfied," Chloe said. "That third run was for me to prove to myself that I did it."

That's exactly what she did. Chloe dropped into the half-pipe and opened with a huge method air—a trick in which the snowboarder grabs the heel edge of their board with their front hand and arches their body backward. Then she uncorked her signature trick: nailing the back-to-back 1080s and finishing with a McTwist flourish. Chloe's 98.25 score on that third run put her almost ten points ahead of the silver medalist—China's Liu Jiayu.

35

As she stood atop the podium and smiled for the cameras with the gold medal around her neck, Chloe told herself, "I can't cry right

now . . . I worked so hard on my eyeliner!" But in the crowd, her parents were crying and cheering. Jong Jin had been right. Today was the day his ipugi had risen to the sky with her big power, claimed the gold medal, and become a dragon. For Jong Jin, watching Chloe win gold was his American dream.

CHAPTER 5
Looking to the Future

After the Olympic Winter Games in South Korea, Chloe returned home to the United States to find that she had become a celebrity. Chloe and her dog, Reese, a mini Australian shepherd, appeared on the cover of *Sports Illustrated* together. And when Kellogg's created a special Corn Flakes box featuring Chloe and her Olympic gold medal, it sold out in seven hours, becoming the fastest-selling cereal box in Kellogg's history. Chloe appeared on talk shows with hosts like Jimmy Fallon and James

Corden. She also won the 2018 ESPY Award for Best Female Athlete, was named one of *TIME* magazine's "100 Most Influential People of 2018" and even appeared in Maroon 5's music video for "Girls Like You."

Slowly, Chloe tried to settle back into regular teenage life. She studied for, and took, the ACT and the SAT and scored well enough to be accepted to her dream school—Princeton University, where she hoped to major in science. In 2019, she won her fifth X Games title and her first world championship gold, extending her unbeaten streak to eight events.

Chloe's winning streak finally snapped in March 2019 when she finished second behind Maddie Mastro at the US Open. She later revealed that she had broken her ankle on her first run and would need surgery to fix it. The injury gave Chloe her first break from competitive snowboarding in years. In October 2019, Chloe decided to extend that time off and take a yearlong break from competition to start her freshman year at Princeton. "When I broke my ankle, it was a very minor fall and it just made me think, 'Wow, my body is tired,'" Chloe said. After years of homeschooling as she traveled the world competing in snowboarding, Chloe was excited to experience life as a "regular" college kid.

Transitioning to college life was hard at first. Chloe had to figure out how to balance all her classes. She realized that she'd never had to sit in a lecture and had to learn how to take notes effectively. But things soon got better, and Chloe found a group of good friends who didn't treat her differently because she was a famous athlete.

In January 2021, Chloe took a leave of absence from Princeton to return to competitive snowboarding and start training for the 2022 Winter Olympics, which will be held in Beijing, China. Was she rusty after her twenty-one-month break from competition? Chloe answered that question definitively by winning the first four events she entered in 2021—the Laax Open World Cup, the X Games, the world championship, and the US Grand Prix.

Heading into the Beijing Olympics, Chloe is still the one to beat in the women's half-pipe. She's hired a trainer to work on her fitness, and she feels stronger and more confident than ever on her snowboard. But even though expectations are high for the reigning half-pipe Olympic gold medalist, Chloe is trying to take everything in stride. "I kind of want to go in with the same approach as I did with the last one," she says. "Just chilling."

Winter Olympics: The Half-Pipe Event

Snowboarding was first included in the Winter Olympics in Nagano, Japan, in 1998. The first two snowboarding events were the parallel giant slalom (snowboarders go through sets of gates spaced along a tall hill) and the half-pipe.

In the Olympics, snowboarders get two attempts, called "runs," to put together their best

sequences of tricks in the qualification round. They are scored on a one-hundred-point scale and receive a score based on the height, difficulty, and execution of their tricks. Their score also reflects how well they link them together and how thoroughly they use the entire half-pipe.

The top twelve snowboarders in the qualification round advance to the final round, where they get three attempts to show off their best runs.

Timeline of Chloe Kim's Life

2000 — Born April 23 in Torrance, California

2004 — Learns to snowboard

2008 — Moves to Geneva, Switzerland, to learn French

2010 — Moves back to the United States and starts training with the Mammoth Mountain snowboarding team

2013 — Goes pro and qualifies for the 2014 Sochi Olympics but is too young to participate

2015 — Wins gold medal at the X Games, becoming the youngest winner in the history of the competition at that time

2016 — At the US Snowboarding Grand Prix, becomes the first woman to land back-to-back 1080s in a competition

2017 — Wins the Dew Tour to qualify for the 2018 PyeongChang Winter Olympics

2018 — Wins a gold medal in the women's half-pipe event at the Winter Olympics, becoming the youngest American woman to ever medal in snowboarding at the Olympics

2019 — Wins her first world championship

— Takes a year off from competitive snowboarding to start her freshman year at Princeton University

2020 — Returns to competitive snowboarding and trains for the 2022 Winter Olympics

2021 — Wins her second world-championship title

Timeline of the World

2000	Hillary Clinton is elected to the United States Senate, becoming the first former First Lady of the United States to win public office
2004	The social networking site known as Facebook is launched
2007	The Great Recession devastates world financial markets
2008	Barack Obama is elected the forty-fourth president of the United States and the nation's first Black president
	At the Beijing Summer Olympics, US swimmer Michael Phelps wins eight gold medals, the most ever won by one athlete in a single Olympic Games
2012	George Zimmerman shoots and kills Trayvon Martin, an unarmed Black teenager, in Florida
2013	The Black Lives Matter movement to protest institutional racism against Black people is launched
2015	Same-sex marriage is federally legalized in the United States
2019	The coronavirus disease COVID-19 is first found in Wuhan, China, and eventually creates a worldwide pandemic
2020	The Tokyo Summer Olympics are postponed to 2021 due to the COVID-19 pandemic
2021	Kamala D. Harris becomes the first female vice president of the United States

Bibliography

*Books for young readers

Kang, Inyoung, and Matt Stevens. "Chloe Kim's Olympic journey started at Mountain High, with her dad." *New York Times*, February 12, 2018. https://www.nytimes.com/2018/02/12/us/california-today-chloe-kim-olympics.html.

*Moon, Derek. *Olympic Stars: Chloe Kim*. North Mankato, Minnesota: Abdo Publishing, 2019.

*Raum, Elizabeth. *Pro Sports Biographies: Chloe Kim*. Mankato, Minnesota: Amicus High Interest, 2018.

Roenigk, Alyssa. "Chloe Kim fulfills her golden destiny, from 'baby girl' to full-fledged dragon." *ESPN.com*, February 13, 2018. https://www.espn.com/olympics/story/_/id/22415338/chloe-kim-fulfills-golden-destiny-halfpipe-baby-girl-full-fledged-dragon.

Roenigk, Alyssa. "Kid Fearless." *ESPN the Magazine*, February 6, 2018. http://www.espn.com/espnw/feature/22265441/snowboard-phenom-chloe-kim-lot-riding-winter-olympics.

Wharton, David. "Chloe Kim and Kelly Clark—the link between snowboarding's past and future." *Los Angeles Times*, March 10, 2020. https://www.latimes.com/sports/story/2020-03-10/chloe-kim-kelly-clark-snowboarding-winter-olympics.